CHANUKAH
& OTHER HEBREW HOLIDAY SONGS

25 of the Best-Known Hebrew & Yiddish Melodies
Arranged for Easy Piano with Lyrics & Guitar Chords

Allan Small

Foreword

Singing is an integral part of all Jewish celebrations and observances. This book contains some of the most beloved Hebrew and Yiddish melodies of all time. Included are music and lyrics celebrating Chanukah, Passover and Purim; traditional melodies for the Sabbath and Yom Kippur; and well-known Israeli and Yiddish folk songs.

Fingering, pedaling and dynamics have been carefully added for ease and precision in performance. Selections have been placed in order of difficulty—the easiest ones at the beginning of the book.

Contents (alphabetical)

Cover design: Martha Widmann
Cover photography: Jeff Oshiro
Music engraving: Nancy Butler
Project editor: Sharon Barasch

Menorah and draydles courtesy of Tina Oberman,
Gallery Judaica, Los Angeles

Contents (categorical)

HOLIDAY SONGS

ISRAELI SONGS

LITURGICAL SONGS/MELODIES

YIDDISH SONGS/MELODIES

Pronounciation Guide

HEBREW

a	as in	tall
ay	as in	play
ai	as in	high
ei	as in	hair
e	as in	led
i	as in	meet
'	as in	lit
o	as in	over
u	as in	boot
ch	as in	Bach
ts, tz	as in	bats

For a more authentic sound, roll r's (either on your tongue or in your throat), and dentalize t's and d's.

YIDDISH

a	as in	tall
ei	as in	may
ai	as in	high
e	as in	led
i	as in	lit
o	as in	mother
oi	as in	boy
u	as in	boot
ch	as in	Bach
ts, tz	as in	bats
zh	as in	pleasure

Various combinations of consonants that we do not have in English, such as "bn," are pronounced simply by forming one consonant after the other.

CHANUKAH

Hebrew

2. Chanukah, Chanukah, ein chalon b'li aysh
   Sufgan' yot, l'vivot b'kol bayit yeish.
   Chanukah, Chanukah, chag chaviv m'od,
   Shiru na, shiru na, utsu na lirkod!

English

1. Chanukah, Chanukah is such a beautiful holiday,
   Lovely light all around brings joy to young children,
   Chanukah, Chanukah, turn, turn the draydl.
   Turn, turn, turn, turn, turn, turn, what a pleasure and delight!

2. Chanukah, Chanukah, no window is without light,
   Donuts and latkes are served in every home.
   Chanukah, Chanukah is a very lovely holiday,
   Sing out, sing out, rush to dance!

DAYEINU
(IT WOULD HAVE BEEN ENOUGH!)

From the Passover Haggadah

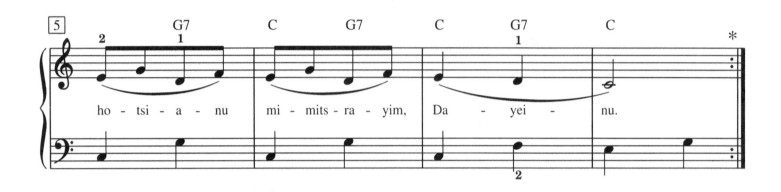

*Optional repeat is for piano solo.

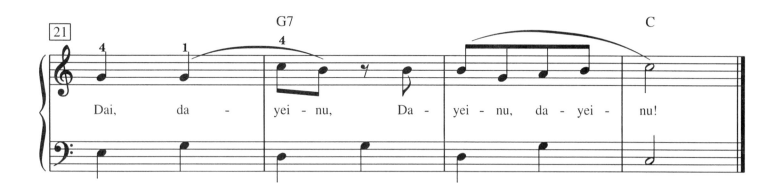

Hebrew

2. Ilu natan, natan lanu, natan lanu et hashabbat
   Natan lanu et hashabbat, dayeinu.
   Dai, dayeinu, *etc.*

3. Ilu natan, natan lanu, natan lanu et hatorah.
   Natan lanu et hatorah, dayeinu.
   Dai, dayeinu, *etc.*

English

1. Had God brought us forth from Egypt—*It would have
   been enough!*

2. Had He given us the Sabbath—*It would have been enough!*

3. Had He given us the Torah—*It would have been enough!*

DRAYDL SONG

For Chanukah

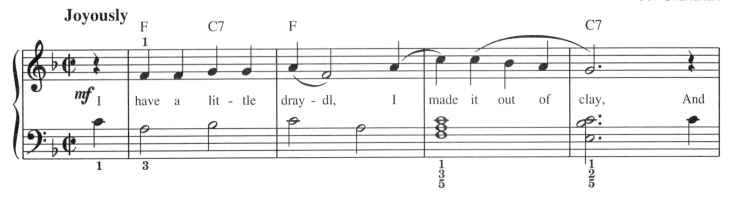

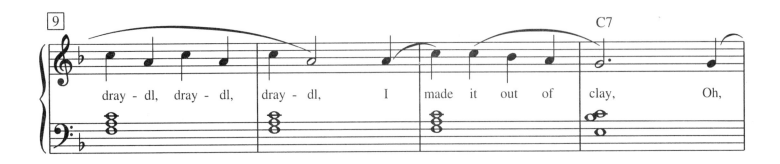

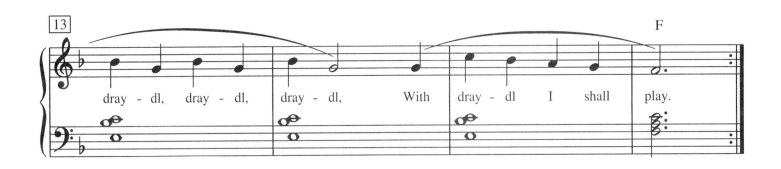

2. It has a lovely body
   With leg so short and thin,
   And when it gets all tired,
   It drops and then I win!
   Chorus

3. My draydl's always playful,
   It loves to dance and spin.
   A happy game of draydl,
   Come play, now let's begin!
   Chorus

CHAG PURIM

(PURIM DAY)

Folk Song

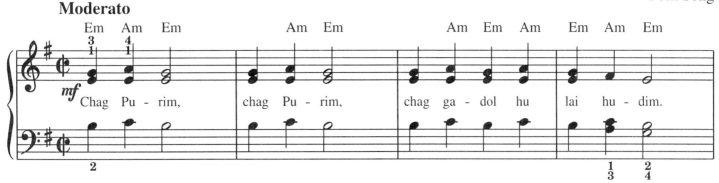

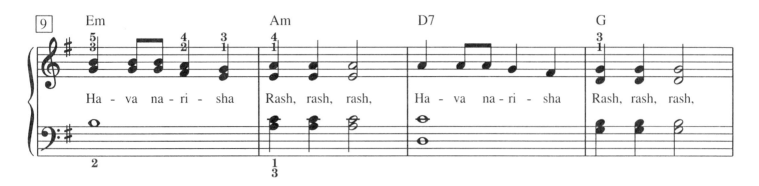

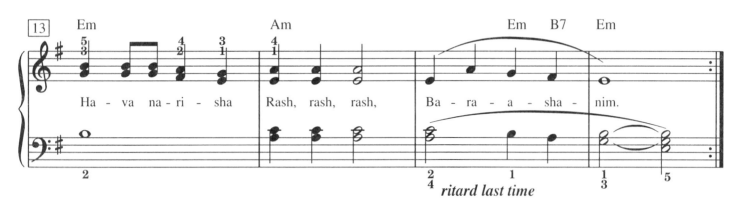

ritard last time

Hebrew

2. Chag Purim, chag Purim,
   Ze el ze sholchim manot,
   Machmadim, mamtakim,
   Tufinim migdanot.

   Hava narisha, *etc.*

English

1. Purim is a festive day for the Jewish people.
   There are masks, *graggers* (noisemakers), songs and dances.
   Chorus: Come let's make a row with the *graggers.*

2. On Purim day we exchange gifts: sweets, cakes,
   and all manner of good things.
   Chorus

HATIKVAH
(THE HOPE)
Also the Israeli National Anthem

N. H. Imber
Adapted from a melody by Smetana

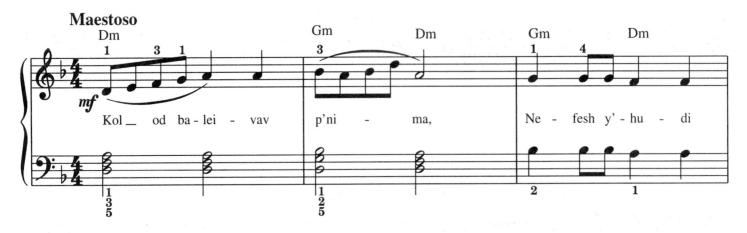

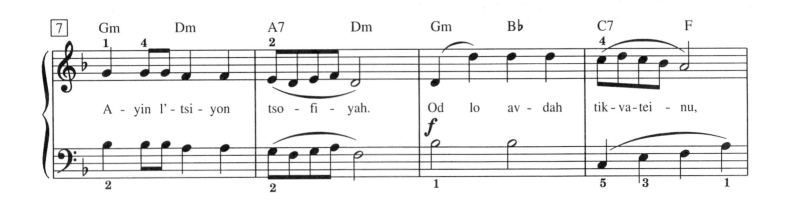

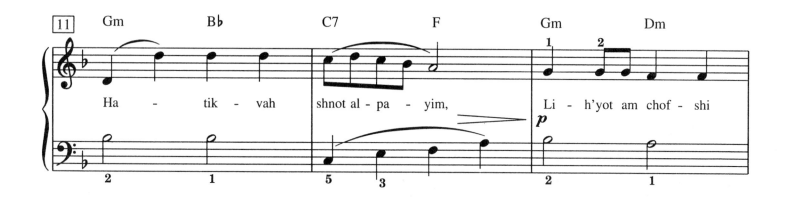

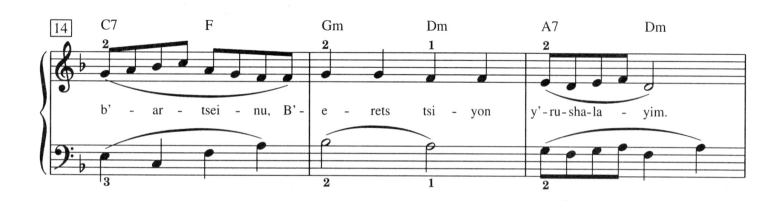

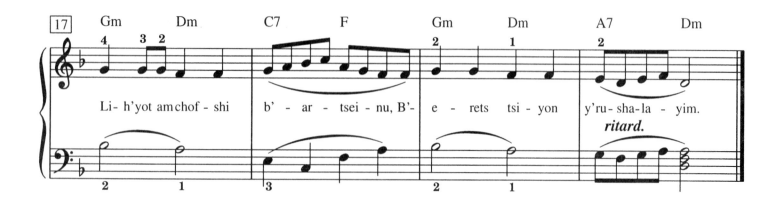

English

So long as the heart of the Jew beats, and his eye is turned to the East—
the ancient hope to return to Zion lives.

OH CHANUKAH

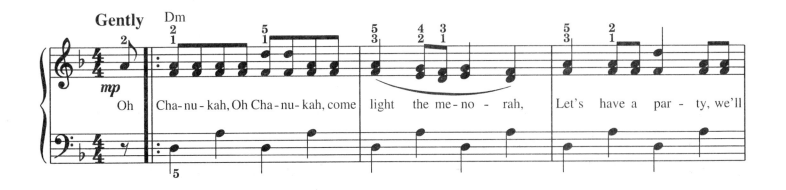

Oh Cha-nu-kah, Oh Cha-nu-kah, come light the me-no-rah, Let's have a par-ty, we'll

all dance the ho-ra, Ga-ther 'round the ta-ble, I'll give you a treat,

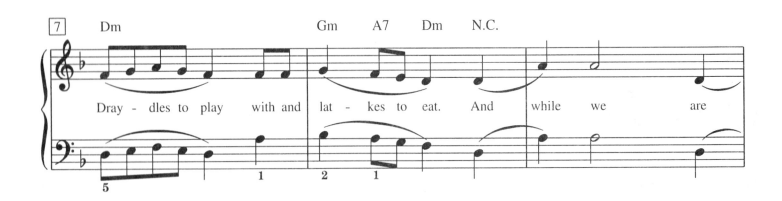

Dray-dles to play with and lat-kes to eat. And while we are

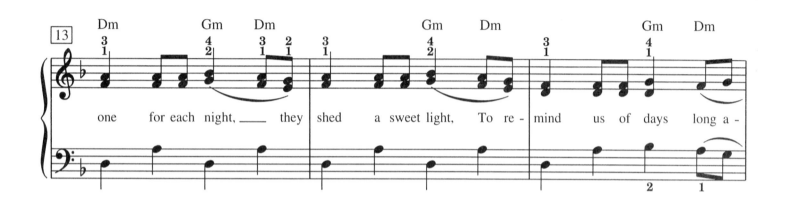

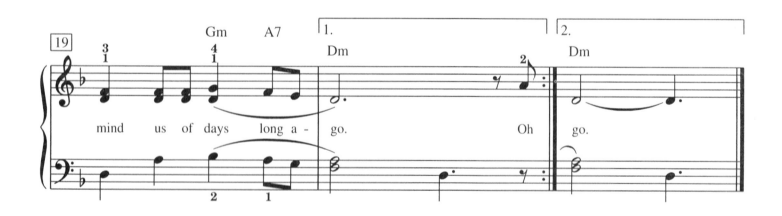

HEIVEINU SHALOM ALAYCHEM

(WE BRING YOU PEACE)

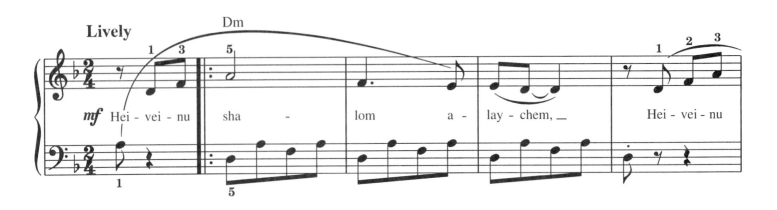

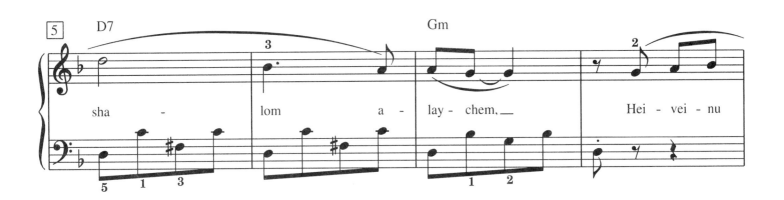

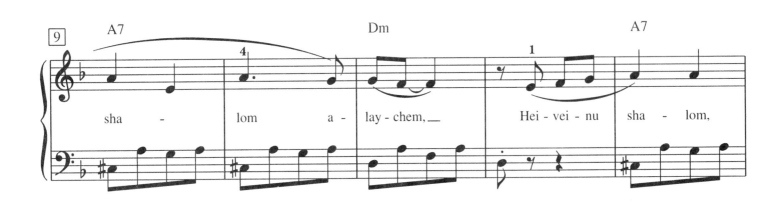

OIF'N PRIPITSHIK

(ON THE FIREPLACE)

Tenderly and rather slowly

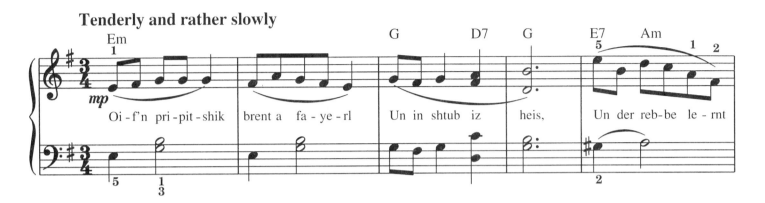

Oi-f'n pri-pit-shik brent a fa-ye-rl Un in shtub iz heis, Un der reb-be le-rnt

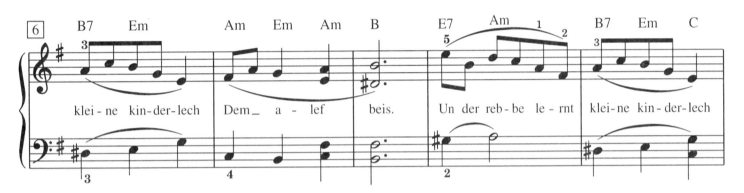

klei-ne kin-der-lech Dem_ a-lef beis. Un der reb-be le-rnt klei-ne kin-der-lech

Chorus

Dem_ a-lef beis. Gedenkt zhe kin-der-lech, Gedenkt zhe ta-ye-re, Vos ir le-rnt

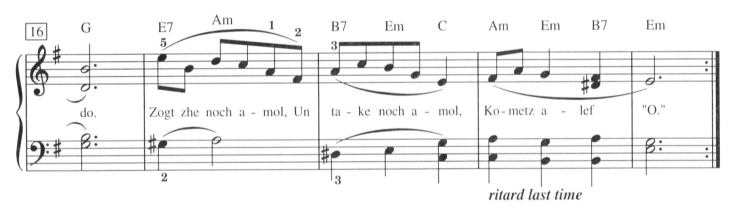

do. Zogt zhe noch a-mol, Un ta-ke noch a-mol, Ko-metz a-lef "O."

ritard last time

English

The teacher's room is warm
From flames burning low
In the fireplace,
And the little ones
Repeat eagerly
The Hebrew alphabet.

Chorus

Study children dear,
Remember, precious ones,
Aw, Baw, Gaw, Daw.
Say it once again,
And then yet again,
Kometz alef "O."

ARTSA ALINU
(WE HAVE COME TO THE LAND)

*One of the songs
of the early chalutzim*

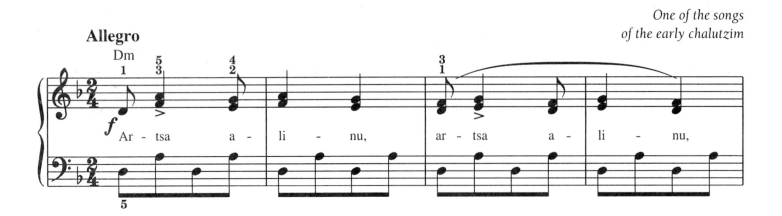

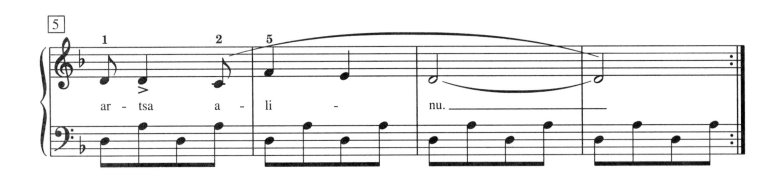

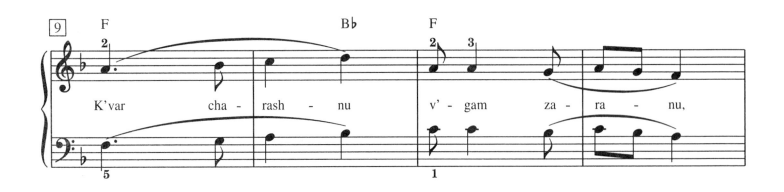

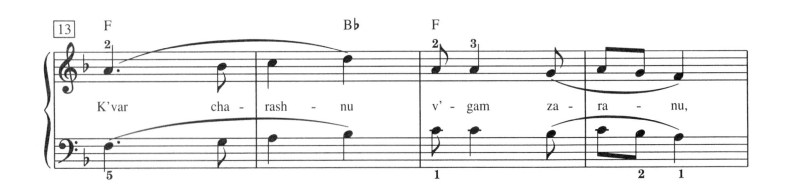

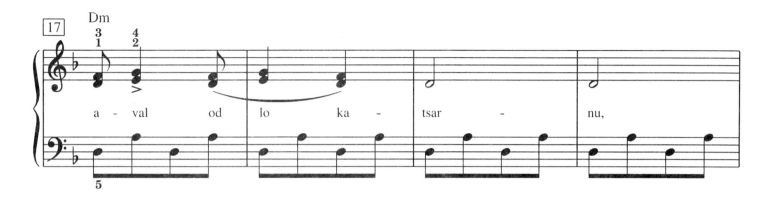

a – val   od   lo   ka –   tsar –   nu,

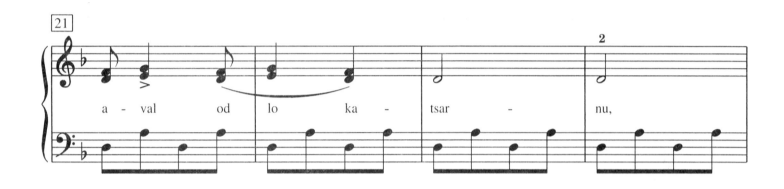

a – val   od   lo   ka –   tsar –   nu,

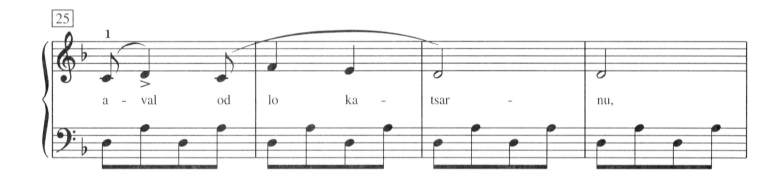

a – val   od   lo   ka –   tsar –   nu,

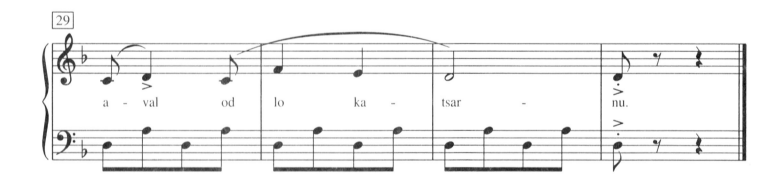

a – val   od   lo   ka –   tsar –   nu.

English

We have come to the Land of Israel. We have already plowed and sown,
but we have not yet harvested.

HAVA NAGILA
(Let Us Rejoice)

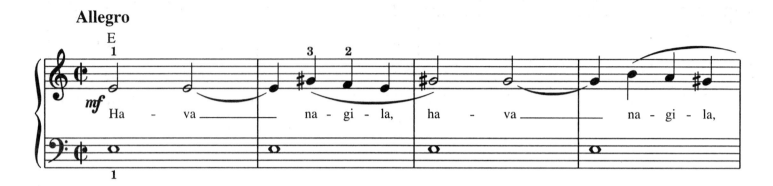

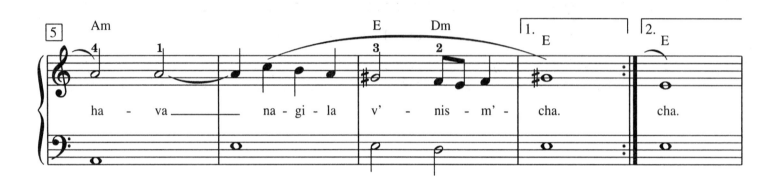

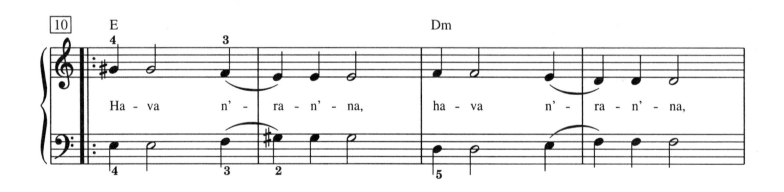

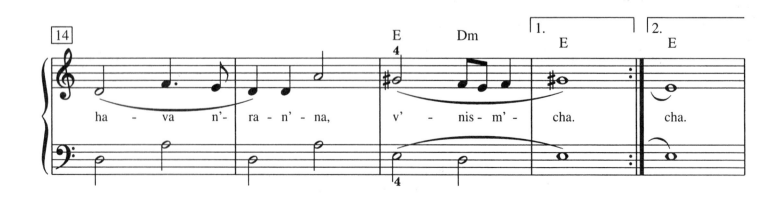

English
Let us rejoice and be happy. Let us sing and be happy.
Stir yourselves, brethren, with a happy heart.

SHALOM ALAYCHEM

(PEACE UNTO YOU)

Traditionally sung on Friday evening
at the beginning of the Sabbath

Sha - lom a - lay - chem, ma - la - chay ha - sha – reit, ma - la - chay el -

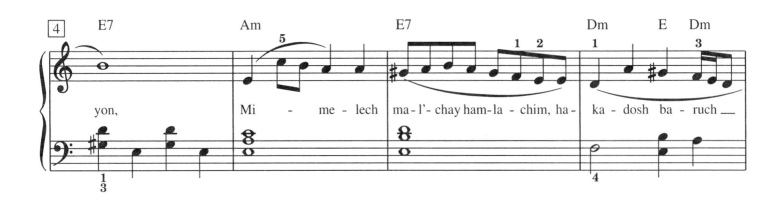

yon, Mi - me - lech ma - l'- chay ham - la - chim, ha - ka - dosh ba - ruch __

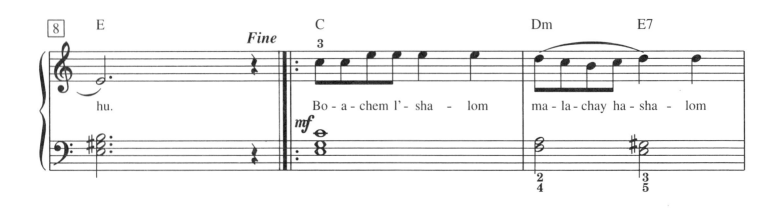

hu.   Bo - a - chem l'- sha - lom ma - la - chay ha - sha - lom

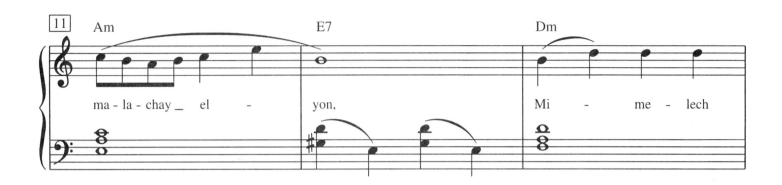

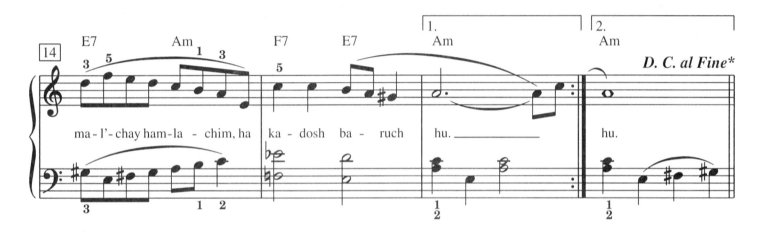

*Go back to the beginning and play until *Fine;* optional repeats are for piano solo.

Hebrew

2. Barchuni l'shalom malachay hashalom malachay elyon,
    Mimelech malachay hamlachim, hakadosh baruch hu.
    Tseitchem l'shalom malachay hashalom, malachay elyon,
    Mimelech malachay hamlachim hakadosh baruch hu.

English

1. Peace upon you, O ministering angels,
    Angels of the Exalted One, King of kings,
    The Holy One, blessed be He.

2. May your coming be for peace,
    Angels of the Exalted One, King of kings,
    The Holy One, blessed be He.

LOMIR ZICH IBERBETN

(LET'S MAKE UP)

Plaintively

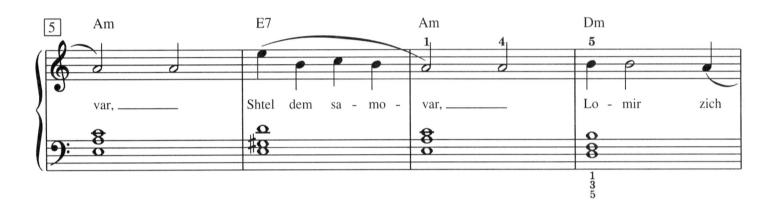

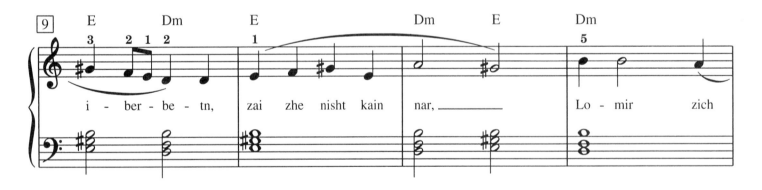

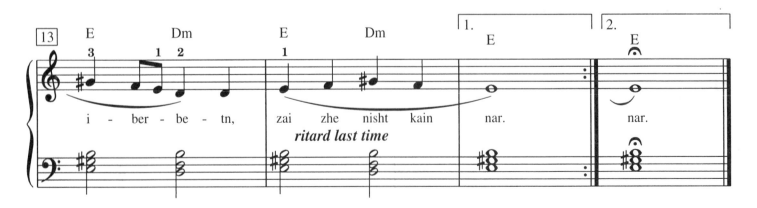

English
Let's make up—set the samovar, and don't be silly.

MI CHAMOCHA?

(WHO IS LIKE UNTO YOU?)

From the Prayer Book

* "Adoshem" is used to represent "Adonai" when sung in a non-religious setting.

English
Who is like unto You, O Lord, among the mighty?
Who is like unto You, glorious in holiness, revered in praises, doing wonders?

AHZ DER REBBE ELIMELECH
(Rabbi Elimelech)

Rhythmically

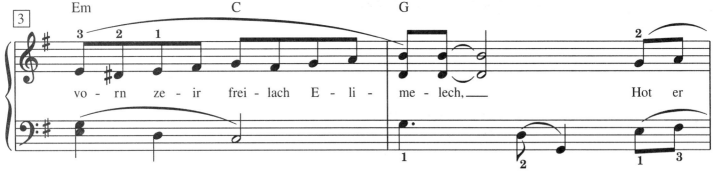

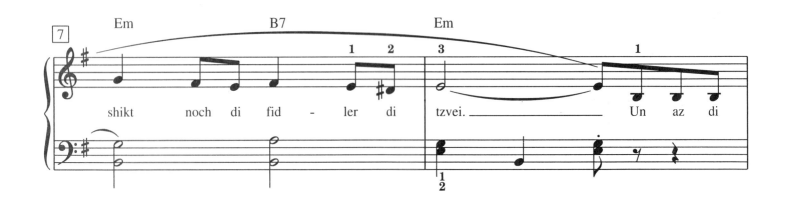

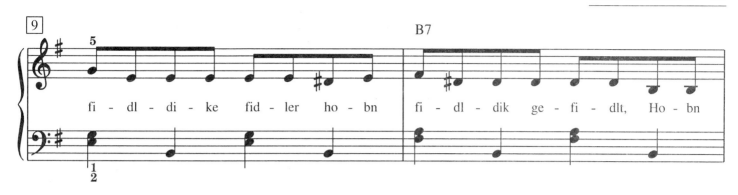

fi – dl – di – ke   fid – ler   ho – bn   fi – dl – dik   ge – fi – dlt,   Ho – bn

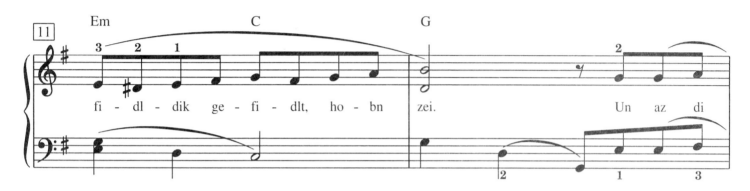

fi – dl – dik   ge – fi – dlt,   ho – bn   zei.   Un   az   di

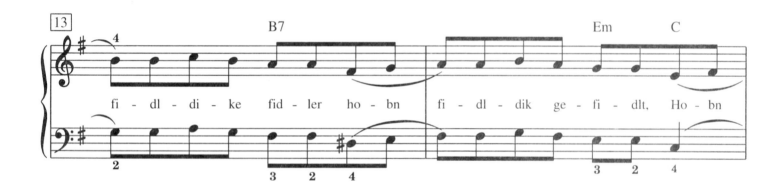

fi – dl – di – ke   fid – ler   ho – bn   fi – dl – dik   ge – fi – dlt,   Ho – bn

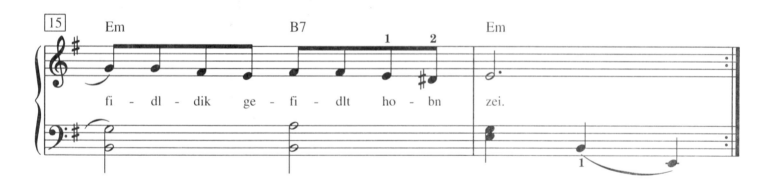

fi – dl – dik   ge – fi – dlt   ho – bn   zei.

Yiddish

2. Un az der Rebbe Elimelech
    Iz gevorn gor shtark freilach,
    Iz gevorn gor shtark freilach Elimelech,
    Hot er oisgeton dem kitl,
    Un hot ongeton dos hitl,
    Un geshikt noch di paikler di tzvei.
    Un az di paikldike paikler hobn paikldik gepaiklt,
    Hobn paikldik gepaiklt, hobn zei.

English

1. When Rabbi Elimelech became very happy. . .
    he completed the *Havdalah* service (the prayer ushering
    out the Sabbath) with his sexton, Reb Naftole, and sent
    for the fiddlers two.
    And the fiddlers fiddled away. . .

2. And when Rabbi Elimelech became even more happy. . .
    he took off his white cloak and put on his walking hat,
    and sent for the drummers two.
    And the drummers drummed away. . .

TUM-BALALAIKA

(PLAY, BALALAIKA)

Moderato

Shteit   a   bo - cher   un ____ er   tracht,

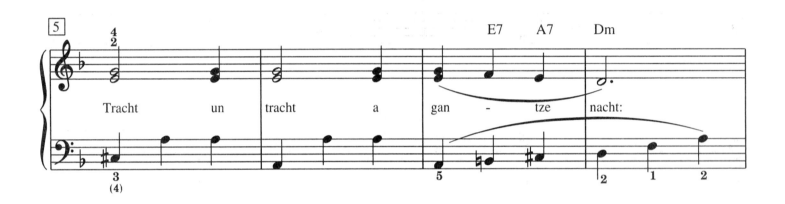

Tracht   un   tracht   a   gan - tze   nacht:

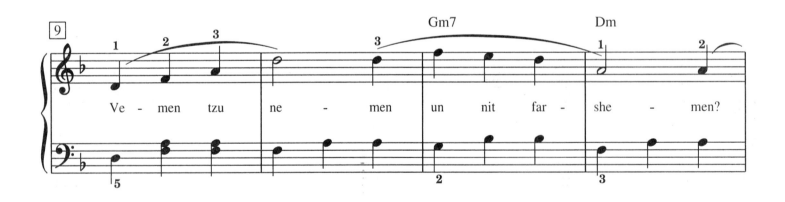

Ve - men   tzu   ne - men   un   nit   far - she - men?

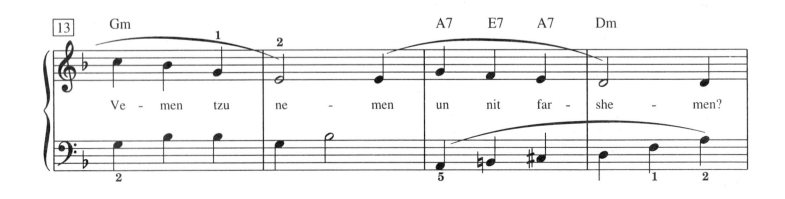

Ve - men   tzu   ne - men   un   nit   far - she - men?

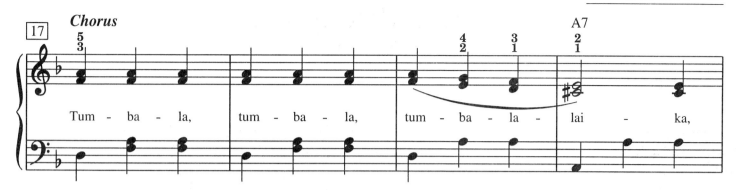

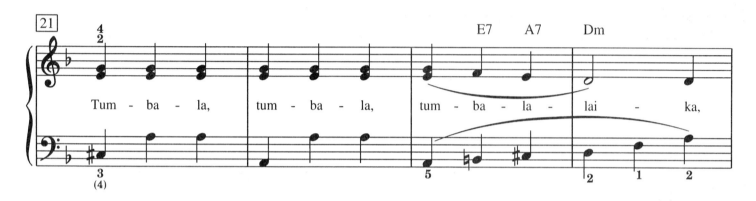

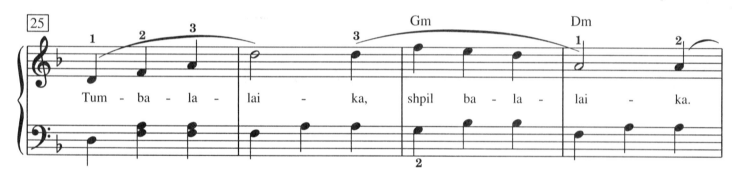

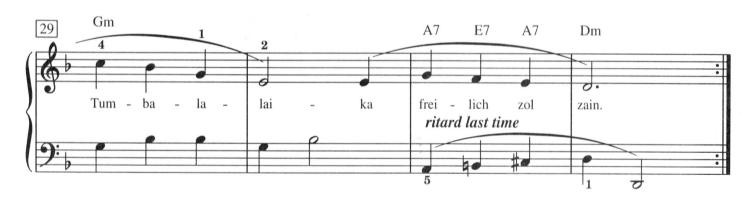

Yiddish

2. Meidl, meidl, ch'vil bai dir fregn:
   Vos kon vaksn, vaksn on regn?
   Vos kon brenen un nit oifhern?
   Vos kon benken, veinen on trern?
Chorus

3. Narisher bocher, vos darfstu fregn?
   A shtein kon vaksn, vaksn on regn.
   Libe kon brenen, un nit oifhern.
   A hartz kon benken, veinen on trern.
Chorus

English

1. A young man stands, engrossed in thought—he thinks and thinks the
   whole night through: Whom do I choose. . . and not break any hearts?
Chorus: Tum-Balalaika, play Balalaika.

2. Maiden, maiden, I've questions to ask you: What can grow
   without rain? What can burn and not cease? What can yearn and
   weep without tears?
Chorus

3. Foolish young man, why do you ask? A stone can grow without
   rain. Love can burn and not cease. A heart can yearn and weep
   without tears.
Chorus

ROZHINKES MIT MANDLEN

(Raisins and Almonds)

Slowly and tenderly

In dem beis ha - mik - dash, In a vin - kl chei - der,

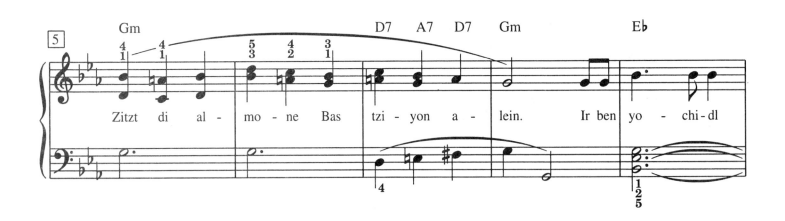

Zitzt di al - mo - ne Bas tzi - yon a - lein. Ir ben yo - chi - dl

Yi - de - le Vigt zi ke - sei - der, Un zingt im zum shlo - fn A

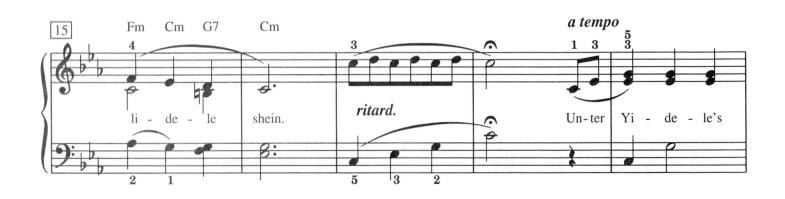

li - de - le shein.   *ritard.*   *a tempo*   Un - ter Yi - de - le's

vi - ge - le (echo) Shteit a klor vais tzi - ge -

le. (echo) Dos tzi-ge-le iz ge - fo - rn han - dlen,

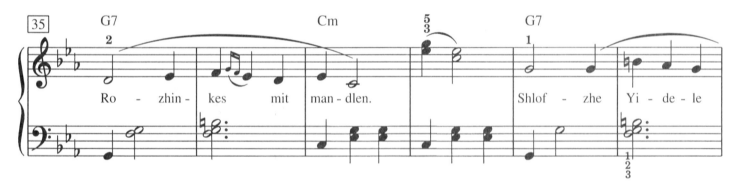

Dos vet zain dain be - ruf. (echo)

Ro - zhin - kes mit man - dlen. Shlof - zhe Yi - de - le

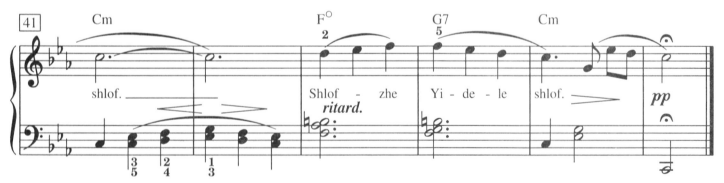

shlof. ____ Shlof - zhe Yi - de - le shlof.
ritard. pp

English

In a corner of the ancient sanctuary sits the widowed Daughter of Zion alone.
Her only child, Yidele, she rocks gently, and sings him a lullaby:
Under Yidele's crib stands a white billygoat. The goat went to market.
That's what you will do one day. Raisins and almonds. . . Sleep, Yidele, sleep.

REB DOVIDL
(Rabbi David)

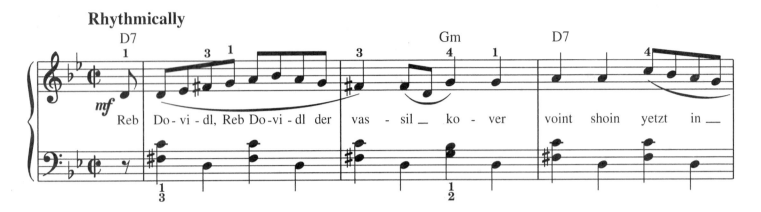

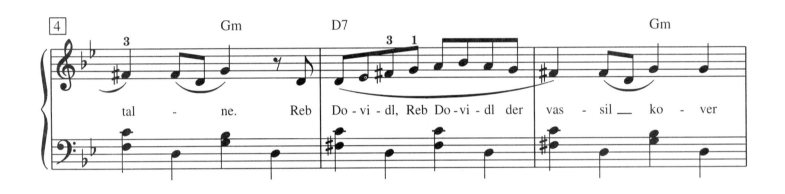

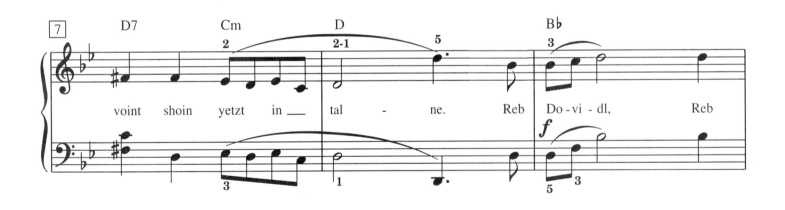

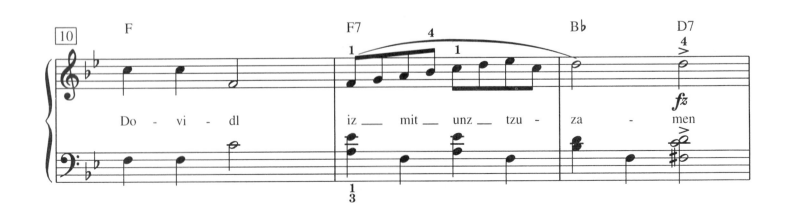

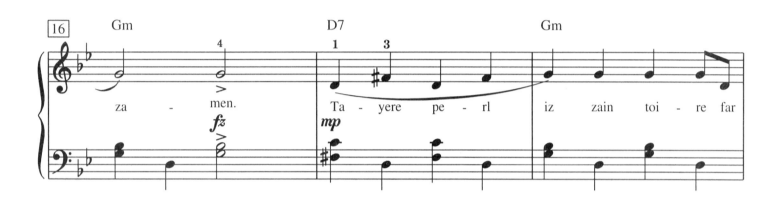

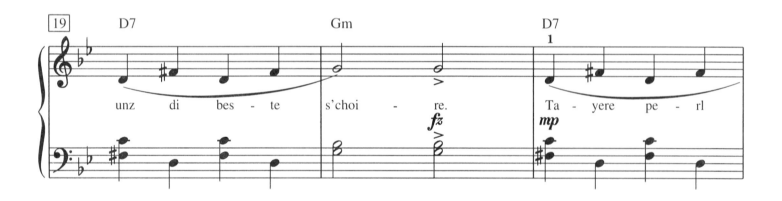

English
Beloved Rabbi David from Vasilkove now resides in Talne. Come quickly to his table so you'll not miss his words of *Torah* (the law). His *Torah* is like precious pearls, the best of all treasures.

BIZTU MIT MIR BROIGEZ?

(ARE YOU ANGRY WITH ME?)

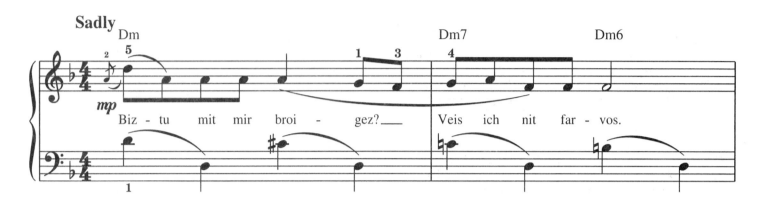

Biz - tu mit mir broi - gez?___ Veis ich nit far - vos.

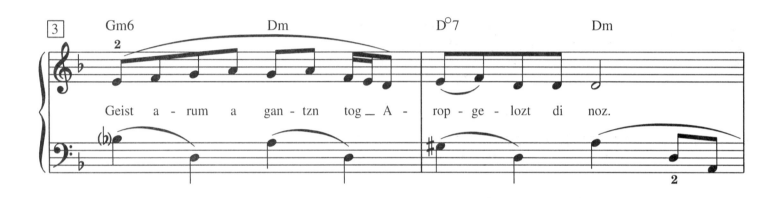

Geist a - rum a gan - tzn tog___ A - rop - ge - lozt di noz.

Ta di - dai, dai - dai - dai, ta di - dai, dai.

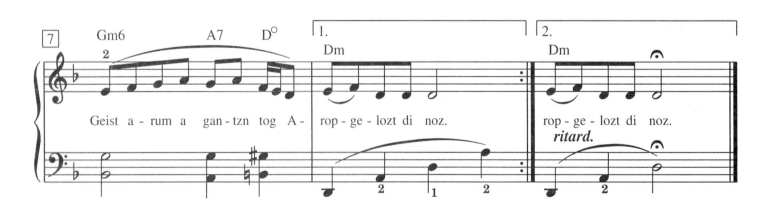

Geist a - rum a gan - tzn tog A - rop - ge - lozt di noz.   rop - ge - lozt di noz.

ritard.

English
Are you angry with me? I don't know why.
You mope around all day with a long face.

OT AZOI NEIT A SHNAIDER

(THIS IS THE WAY A TAILOR SEWS)

* Go back to the beginning and play until Fine.

Yiddish

Chorus

2. A shnaider neit un neit un neit,
    Un hot kadoches, nit kain broit!

Chorus

English

Chorus: This is the way a tailor sews, this is the way he sews!

He sews and sews the whole week long, and earns a penny with a hole in it!
Chorus

A tailor sews and sews and sews, and has but misery to show for it!
Chorus

SH'MA YISRAEIL

(HEAR, O ISRAEL)

From the Prayer Book

Maestoso

Sh'ma Yisra-eil a-do-shem* e-lo-hay-nu a-do-shem e-chad.

Fine

Sh'ma Yisra-eil a-do-shem e-lo-hay-nu a-do-shem e-chad.

D. C. al Fine**

ritard.

* "Adoshem" is used to represent "Adonai" when sung in a non-religious setting.

**Go back to the beginning and play until Fine.

English
Hear, oh Israel, the Lord our God, the Lord is one.

YISRAEIL V'ORAITA

(ISRAEL AND THE TORAH)

* Go back to the beginning and play until Fine.

English
Israel and the Torah are one. The Torah is light.
Halleluyah! Praise the Lord!

MAOZ TSUR
(ROCK OF AGES)

Chanukah hymn
English version from the Union Hymnal

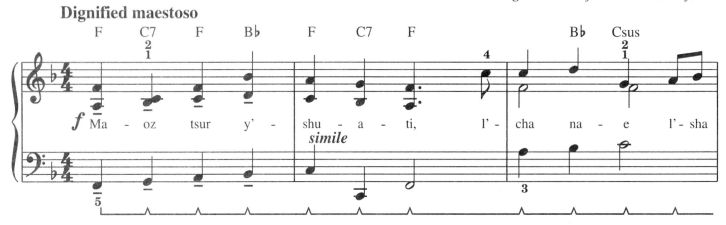

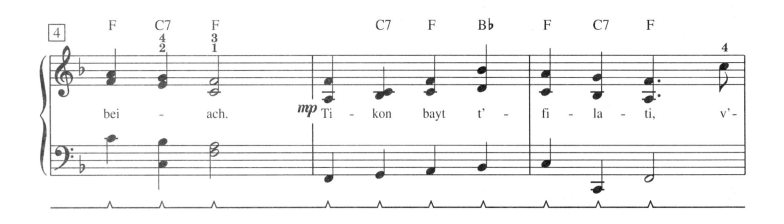

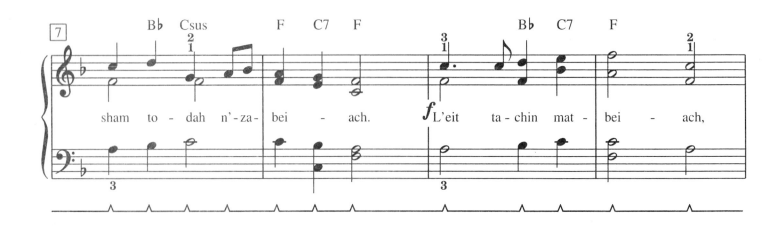

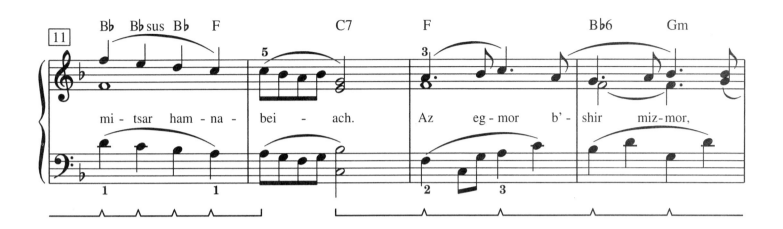

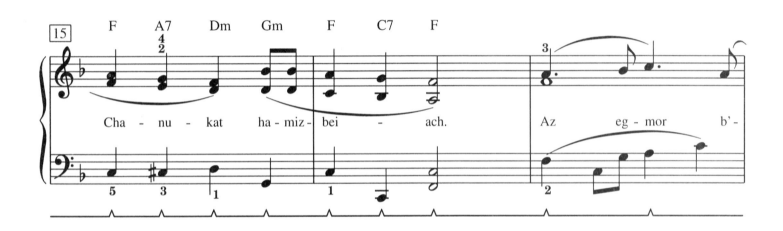

English

Rock of Ages, let our song
Praise Thy saving power;
Thou amidst the raging foes,
Wast our shelt'ring tower.
Furious they assailed us,

But Thine arm availed us,
And Thy word
Broke their sword
When our own strength failed us.

FRAYLOCH

(Happiness)

*Go back to the beginning and play until the Coda ⊕ sign, then skip to the Coda.

KOL NIDRE
(ALL VOWS)

Largo espressivo

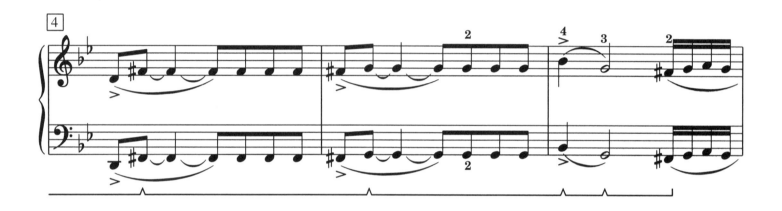

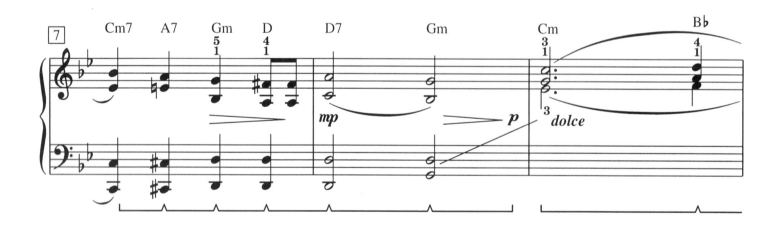

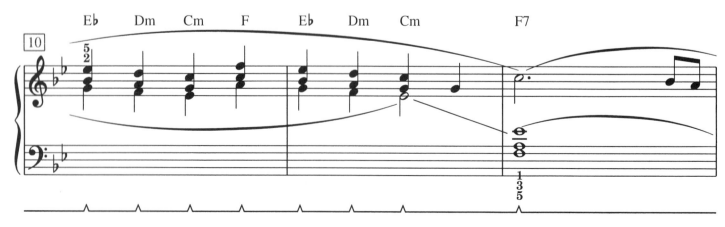

*As this piano piece is based on the widely known melody of "Kol Nidre" and is not a direct transcription, lyrics are omitted.

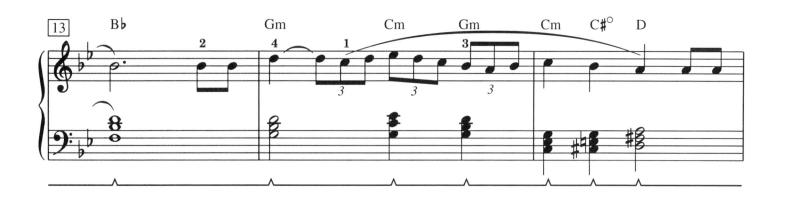

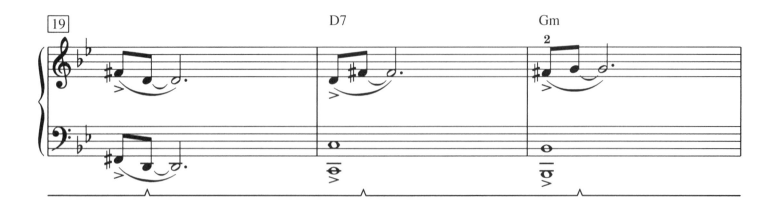

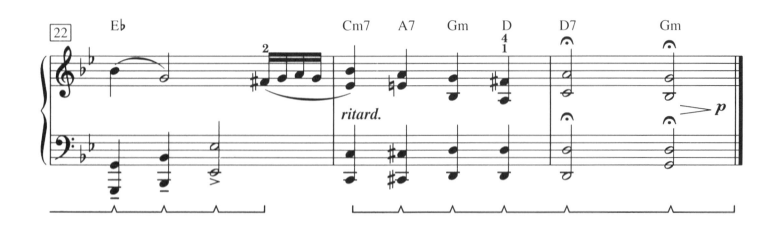

AVINU MALKEINU
(OUR FATHER, OUR KING)

From the Prayer Book for High Holy Days

English
Our Father, our King, be gracious unto us and answer us, for we are
wanting in good deeds. Deal with us in charity and kindness, and save us.